John Townsend's

Tickling with Words

Creatures, teachers & cheesy queasy features

I finished reading this book on:

............/............/............

Illustrated by Stef Murphy

BOOK HOUSE
a SALARIYA imprint

Contents

1821   FEB 2018

JO

Renfrewshire
Council

The library is always open at
renfrewshirelibraries.co.uk

Visit now for
homework help
and free
eBooks.

We are the Skoobs and we love the library!

Phone: 0300 300 1188
Email: libraries@renfrewshire.gov.uk

Dedicated to word-ticklers everywhere.

JT

Published in Great Britain in MMXVIII by
Book House, an imprint of
The Salariya Book Company Ltd
25 Marlborough Place, Brighton BN1 1UB
www.salariya.com

ISBN: 978-1-912006-65-6

SALARIYA

Text © John Townsend MMXVIII
© The Salariya Book Company Ltd MMXVIII

1 3 5 7 9 8 6 4 2

A CIP catalogue record for this book is available
from the British Library.
Printed and bound in China.
Printed on paper from sustainable sources.

Editor: Jacqueline Ford
Assistant editor: Nick Pierce
Designer: Mark Williams

Visit
www.salariya.com
for our online catalogue and
free fun stuff.

PAPER FROM
SUSTAINABLE
FORESTS

Author:
John Townsend worked as a secondary school teacher before becoming a full-time writer. He specialises in illuminating and humorous information books for all ages.

Artist:
Stef Murphy is a graduate of Loughborough University and now works as a professional illustrator.

Tickling with Words

Introduction

Including cautionary verse
for the nasty, naughty and nutty

'Words are power', it has to be said,
When spoken aloud or quietly read...
They can make you feel sad, astounded or proud
Or tickle a smile – to CHUCKLE OUT LOUD.
Enjoy a quick snicker and tickly big giggle,
As you snigger and titter and jiggle and wriggle...

**There's no need for tickles with feathers from birds,
Just giggle and wriggle and tickle with words!**

Crazy creatures

It isn't much fun as a Werewolf

It isn't much fun as a werewolf
I get quite a lot of complaints
When I nip out at night in a shaft of moonlight
Into Tesco… and somebody faints.
I'm misunderstood as a werewolf;
Each night I must go on the prowl…
In late afternoon I sneak out with the moon
When I can't help but holler and…
HOOOOOWL!

It isn't much fun as a werewolf
I'm out at unsociable hours
Just stalking the woods and dark neighbourhoods
Controlled by the moon and its powers.
I'm misunderstood as a werewolf;
I'm stared at a lot in the street
When hair on my chest bursts out through my vest
And dirty great claws from my feet…
HOOOOOWL!

It isn't much fun as a werewolf
It costs me a fortune at Boots
On face-fur remover, a nostril-hair hoover
And something to lighten my roots… (all over)
I'm misunderstood as a werewolf;
The dentist is always aghast
At slime on my fangs as it slobbers and hangs
And I empty the waiting room fast…
HOOOOOWL!

It isn't much fun as a werewolf
When I go to the library for help
For a book about shaving, then I start misbehaving
And leap on the shelves with a yelp.
I'm misunderstood as a werewolf;
The librarian said I'm grotesque.
She shouted with diction,
"You've weed in nonfiction
And buried a bone by my desk!"
HOOOOOWL!

It isn't much fun as a werewolf
As I make late night shoppers upset
When I rip off my shirt and roll in the dirt
And froth from the mouth at sunset.
I'm misunderstood as a werewolf;
And I've been so unlucky in love
For no one will kiss me with my face always bristly
As I shriek at the full moon above…
HOOOOOWL!

It isn't much fun as a werewolf
When I really don't feel in the mood
For hunting fresh meat late at night in the street
And I like vegetarian food.
I'm misunderstood as a werewolf;
I'm not a carnivorous beast...
As I love cheese on toast or a tofu nut roast
And a tin of baked beans is a feast...
HOOOOOWL!

I'd kill for a veggie burger!

It isn't much fun as a werewolf
I get quite a lot of abuse
Kids on the school bus call me names and they fuss…
When I bite back – and I've got no excuse
Except… I'm misunderstood as a werewolf;
Kids don't understand me at all,
Nor the bus driver when I dribble saliva
Then throw my head back as I bawl…
HOOOOOWL!

It isn't much fun as a werewolf
I daren't leave the house before dark
But skulk in my bed with my eyes glowing red
As I snarl, growl, wail, bellow and bark
HOORAY! I've been cured as a werewolf!
I won't tell you when, where or how;
Enough just to say – I feel human today…
Back to normal – I'm fine again
NOOOOOOOW!

The end

My Big Bad Sister

My big bad sister bites and kicks
And spits at nuns or vicars.
She pokes her tongue at teachers, too.
Her cold stare never flickers.
She yells and rants, then waves her pants
And shouts, "Look at my knickers!"

She pours cold porridge in my shoes,
She's spiteful all the time,
She dangles maggots on my face,
Now surely that's a crime.
I find pink custard in my bed,
She fills my pants with slime.

Last week she found the treacle tin
And poured it down the sink.
We had to phone up Dyno-Rod
And she was tickled pink,
For as the man got out of his van
She squirted him with ink.

Stop laughing or
I'll THROW something...
like another tantrum.

She shouts at people on the news
And throws things at the telly
Or splats the screen with bubblegum
Or fills my socks with jelly.
She'll stuff the fridge with frogs and slugs
Or something very smelly.

She'll hide a mouse-trap in your bath
Or in your soup, a spider,
Or superglue the toilet seat
(For that I can't abide her)
I won't say more, but I'm quite sure
She put mothballs in Dad's cider.

She tears her clothes when tantrums strike
If someone starts to tease her.
She'll throw her tights across the room
And nobody can please her.
She'll widdle in the wheelie bin
Or next door neighbour's freezer.

My Big Bad Sister

My sister sometimes stays in bed
Till way past half eleven.
No KitKats clog the toaster then,
When she's asleep – it's heaven!
You'd never know she's grown up, though…
She's almost thirty-seven!
(And a deputy headteacher)

The end

It isn't much fun as a Vampire

It isn't much fun as a vampire
My job is a pain in the neck.
It's the same every night – I must go for a bite,
If I don't get some blood, I'm a wreck.
I get so distressed as a vampire
As my dentist has strong garlic breath,
When I took tranquilisers, he removed my incisors
Now my prey – I must suck them to death.

It isn't much fun as a vampire

It isn't much fun as a vampire
My bite's not as bad as my bark
I'm grumpy and ratty as, though it sounds batty,
I'm really afraid of the dark.
I get so distressed as a vampire,
I've become such a stick-in-the mud
For I hate eating out, chasing flesh all about
And I faint at the first sight of blood.

It isn't much fun as a vampire
When you haven't got Dracula's fangs
And it isn't fantastic when your knicker elastic
Gets caught in mid-flight, then it twangs.
I'm misunderstood as a vampire
In the crypt upside-down from a girder,
Hanging lifeless all day before hunting for prey…
Yes, life as a vampire is MURDER.

The end

It isn't much fun as a Zombie

It isn't much fun as a zombie
With my dribbling and gurgling and roaring,
As I stare with a stoop, like a right nincompoop...
Between you and me, it's DEAD boring!
I'm misunderstood as a zombie
From my stare, steel scorches and warps,
Or everything freezes from one of my squeezes...
One touch of my hand – you're a corpse.

It isn't much fun as a zombie
With my wheezing from each icy breath
As I drool and I droop like a right nincompoop
With a face that they say looks like death.
I'm misunderstood as a zombie
It's not easy in such a position
As a mind-dead cruel brute in an ill-fitting suit...
In my job as a top politician
(But can you guess who?)

The end

Loopy limericks on crazy creatures

Emu

The emu's a bird from Australia
Not known for attractive regalia.
"It's flightless and ugly,"
A parrot said smugly,
"As a bird, it's a fair dinkum failure."

Fat cat

A scruffy fat cat on the prowl
With a taste for the best waterfowl
Digested one whole...
"What greed!" cried the vole
"A duck-filled-tatty-pus," said the owl.

Maggot

A maggot, on dung, and his brother
Were dining in style with each other
When a bluebottle fly
Landed SPLAT from the sky
"What's that?" they exclaimed. "Oh, it's mother!"

Tortoise

A tortoise drank gas from a trough
Then plodded back home with a cough
Which ignited a blast...
And travelled so fast
It reached home before it set off.

Cheetah

The fastest land mammal's the cheetah
That can quickly outrun an anteater.
One day in a race
A cheetah made chase...
But the anteater didn't give up and ran like
the wind over a very short distance and
somehow messed up the whole meter!

25

Features (cautionary verse - and worse)

Ghostly Warnings

The night that troubled Mr. Clark
Was Halloween – just after dark,
When children spot-on half past four
Came 'Trick or Treating' at his door.
He couldn't bear to hear the knock,
Those squeals and WHOOOAAAAs by five o'clock.
The cheeky taunts to make him scared
Produced a smirk – he was prepared...
Flicking wide his letter box
He fired out sopping, smelly socks.
"No treats are here!" he crossly mocked
As some poor child got duly socked.
Then next he squirted jets of slime
While shouting "CLEAR OFF!" all the time.
"I'll give you tricks," he hissed, then chose
His high-speed, max-strength pressure hose.
"You might be young and very little
But I'll knock you over like a skittle!"
Water sprayed and stung their legs
As next he pelted them with eggs.

Flour bombs flew – he got a strike
And knocked a werewolf off her bike.
Then next a stink bomb landed SPLAT!
On a witch's broom and cat.
"You'll not scare me," he squealed and flung
A steaming splodge of farmyard dung.
The ghostly sheets, now smudged with stains
Were blasted next with sludge from drains
To frantic yelling, screams and bleats…
As frenzied ghosts ripped off their sheets.
"Leave me in peace, is all I ask,"
He splattered paint at every mask,
Purples, reds and yucky greens…
"How I hate these Halloweens.
This'll stop your ghoulish pranks!"
He paused but somewhere in the ranks
Someone sniggered… and he SNAPPED.
"Right – that's it – you'll all be zapped…"

His hand reached up to flick the switch
To decimate each ghost and witch.
A trapdoor opened in the wall
From which shot out a cannonball.
Across the road at sixty-eight,
The blast destroyed the whole front gate
Before demolishing the door,
Plus sixty-six and sixty-four.
From his trapdoor gurgles blurted...
Boiling bubbling blubber spurted
Followed by a sludgy paste
Of luminous atomic waste.
As if that wasn't quite enough,
Mr. Clark got rather tough
And turned a tap beside the door
Which hissed as smoke rose from the floor
Beside the doorstep where, alas
There hung a cloud of mustard gas.
Liquid sprayed from every side...
Just a rinse of cyanide.
He sniggered, fiendishly inspired,
As next a hail of missiles fired
Fuses smoking, all alight,
Detonating dynamite.

Ghostly Warnings

And as he screamed, "Now scarper off!"
He reached for his Kalashnikov.
"I'll give you trick or treat," he barked
As the cat flap smoked and sparked.
Instead of treats like lemonades
He hurled out fizzing hand grenades.

And just to make the children certain
He drew right back the front door curtain
To reveal a shining dome
"This might make you clear off home.
And don't come back, that's my advice."
He launched his nuclear device
Which cleared his front doorstep a treat
As well as wiping out the street.
So when the smoke cleared very late
There was no sign of the estate.
No 'trick or treaters' could be seen…
Such a peaceful Halloween!

Children…
If you now feel too much fear
To 'trick or treat' another year,
Remember that you must beware,
As Mr Clark is still out there
Waiting just behind his wall
For ghouls and ghosts in sheets to call.

So if these fears give sleepless nights
And if you dread such scary frights,
Advice from Mr. Clark is this…
"Try giving Halloween a miss…"
Instead, take heed, reflect and pause…
It might be best to stay indoors.

The end

33

Here LIES Gordon!

When Gordon started telling fibs
His Mum would dig him in the ribs
And sigh, "Oh Gordon, what enormous lies,
Such whoppers for your little size!"
For Gordon, just a tiny youth,
Had no concern to tell the truth.
He didn't care what lies he said...
Whatever came into his head.

At school, a teacher said to him,
"Gordon, where on earth is Jim?
He's missing and it's very weird,
I'm sure he can't have disappeared."
Now Jim was ill at home in bed,
But mischief entered Gordon's head
And so he spun a tragic tale
Of how Jim's Dad had gone to jail!
"He robbed a bank and then got caught…"
Gordon gave a full report
With lots of details, all quite grim
Of stolen cash, some kept by Jim.

Everybody gathered round
To hear the story, all spellbound.
"The story's on the news tonight,"
Gordon lied with great delight.
But later on, the news was blank
On Jim's Dad's plot to rob a bank.
The whole school watched with great surprise
They'd all been told a pack of lies.
Next day they gathered in a throng,
But Gordon shrugged, "I got it wrong.
Misinformed, I think you'll find
Not my fault, so never mind."

The teacher asked, "Just where is Fleur?
Has anybody news of her?"
Gordon knew she had a rash,
But said, "She's had a very nasty crash.
Awful business, six were killed
On the bypass, a tanker spilled
Petrol right across the road
And sparks then made the lot explode.
Fleur was lucky to survive,
Dreadful burns… she's just alive."

The crowd sat round as Gordon lied
They sobbed that Fleur had nearly died.
Within an hour they'd all made cards
To send with flowers and their regards
As well as chocolates in a box
"How nice," Fleur said, with chickenpox.
The class was stunned when she returned,
To see her skin had not been burned.
Instead she just had lots of spots,
"You're very kind – I love you lots."
Her story took the class aback…
"Can we have our chocolates back?"

They flocked round Gordon in a throng,
He shrugged, "Ah well, I got it wrong.
Misinformed, I think you'll find
Not my fault, so never mind."
He smiled as, for a while at least,
Attention to him had increased.
Nothing more did Gordon relish
Than twisting truth that he'd embellish
To the point of utter lies
Just so others watched his eyes,
Hanging on his words for hours
While he held them in his powers.

One afternoon, just after school
At the local swimming pool,
Gordon went with Fleur and Jim
For a nice refreshing swim.
He dived, then rose between his friends,
Complaining that he'd got the bends
By rushing up from off the bottom
But Fleur said, "No, you haven't got 'em
You're only causing a big fuss
To make the lifeguard look at us."

Jim agreed and looked severe,
"We're fed up, Gordon, is that clear?
It's no good fibbing, we assure you,
We've now decided to ignore you."
Gordon stamped his foot until
He kicked it through a metal grille
Far below the waterline
From which he couldn't disentwine.
Pumps and filters churned within
As rotor blades began to spin.
The wave-machine had just begun,
As Gordon's feet were sucked and spun.

He screamed as he was downward dragged,
He waved his arms, his fists he wagged.
He gurgled, spluttered and he roared,
Which, to their word, his friends ignored.
The lifeguard looked across and sighed
At daft pretence of suicide.
"Not again – what silly play!"
She turned around and walked away.
It really was a tiresome prank…
As, for the last time, Gordon sank,
Sucked down to spiralling cascades
And sharp revolving rotor blades.

Jim and Fleur looked down, at last
And saw the bubbles floating past.
Standing hand in hand, they feared,
As through the murky depths they peered.
Telling lies had caused the end
Of Gordon, their dishonest friend.
It didn't take them very long
To shrug and say, "He got it wrong.
Misinformed, we think you'll find...
Not our fault, so never mind."

For underwater, as they'd dreaded,
Gordon and his trunks lay shredded.

The end

Terrifying
teachers -
tales from
School

The School Inspector

I sit at the back of the classroom and watch
All day
It's my job
It's what they expect me to do
And I see all sorts...

I see who sticks chewing gum under the tables and
behind the cupboard
I see who makes rude signs when the teacher's
back is turned
I see who breaks the pencil sharpener and steals
the felt-tip pens
I see who stabs the ink cartridge with a compass
and spatters the floor
I see the grim determination on the faces of those
who want to learn
I see the magic of friendship and the spite in those
who'd destroy it.

The School Inspector

I sit at the back of the classroom and listen
All day
To the chatter and chuckles
Or the silence and concentration
And I hear all sorts...

Tickling with Words

I hear the tapping of pencils and the rattle
of keyboards
I hear the scraping of chairs and the squeak
of pens on whiteboards
I hear the gossip and the giggles and the
prattle and the stories
I hear the frustrated sighs or grinding teeth
in mental arithmetic tests
I hear the 'shshsh' from the teacher and the
'listen very carefullys'
I hear the quiet sobs of the boy who can
never get things right.

I sit at the back of the classroom
and think all day
I think about all I see and hear
I think about what I feel
And I feel all sorts...

I feel sad at unkind and negative words
I feel pleased when bullying is melted by encouragement
I feel joy when I see trust and belief flourish
I feel thrilled at the real excitement of learning
I feel amazed at what growing self-esteem can achieve
I feel hope when measuring stops and inspiring starts.

The School Inspector

At break time they begin to notice me
They offer me their crisps or poke their fingers
   with sniggers.
Many come close and some whisper secrets in
   my ear.
Yes, I see and hear and feel so much...
As the gerbil in the cage at the back of Class 4.

The end

The School Play

Tonight's the night we've practised for,
And now it's come at last.
We've been rehearsing every night;
I'm a member of the cast.
Our school does plays each Christmas term
But this one's best and bigger.
And though I've never starred before,
I'm a most important figure.
Miss told me I'm so talented
My acting is an art.
She only took one look at me
And said I looked the part.

I'm feeling really nervous now.
My knees have got the shakes
But Miss said I would be a star,
I've got just what it takes.
I might get spotted by the press
Or signed-up by T.V.
It's so important I act well
If Drama School's for me.
They're putting on their make-up now
Though I don't have to worry,
It's not part of my character
Besides, I'm in a hurry…

The School Play

I'd better put my costume on
And focus on my role.
It takes great concentration powers...
We actors bear our soul.
We've got three nights of this, you know
It's all-important training...
Performances demand my all
They're mentally so draining.
So off I go to tread the boards,
My public wants me now.
Enjoy the show – and watch my art...
As the back end of the cow.

The end

Kerfuffle and custard
My very first school dinner
(many years ago)

Like trembling Oliver Twist, I gingerly held up my plate.
Mrs Middleditch glared down, her ladle poised,
Her steaming dishcloth seeping stewed soggy cabbage,
Her stained cook's overalls oozing lardy mutton broth.

Kerfuffle and custard

Her eyes were as cold and hard as her dumplings.
Her greasy cheeks glistened like her slushy
  globules of mushy sprouts.
Her brow creased like the crusty crinkled scabby
  skin on her grubby grey custard.
Her double chin wobbled like her saggy lumpy
  squelchy blancmange.

Boiled haddock slopped onto the plate – still
  swimming in watery green something-or-other.
Puddles of red vinegar from chunks of slimy
  beetroot curdled kaleidoscopically.
A plop of mashed spud dotted with brown furry
  clumps dolloped on top.
Colourful… nutritious… GROSS!
Then pudding.
Sludgy semolina swam in a sloppy porridge of
  slippery prunes.
I gulped. "Please, Miss. Can I have just a bit less?"
Gasp… shock… horror… LESS?

The Headmaster was summoned from his roast beef.
"What an ungrateful wretch!
What about children in need?
What you will do is stay right here until you eat
   every single scrap.
You will not leave the table until the plate
   is spotless.
You will be grateful.
You will learn."

He was right.
I learned a lot that day.
Like how to clean a plate – by knocking over a
jug of water...
And in all the kerfuffle of cascading custard
I secretly stuffed fishy-beetrooty-slushy-sludge
into Maxine Filipek's satchel.
Spotless plate,
Job done,
Out to play. Yay!

The end

Mrs. Henderson
(My Teaching Assistant)

They all say I've got problems,
It's in my school report
So they sent in Mrs. Henderson.
They call her my 'Support'.
Although she sits right next to me,
I prefer it on my own.
Her hair gets greyer by the day
(Not all of it's her own).
She's meant to stick right by me
Every minute of each day…
I play a game at dinner time
Called 'Escape From My T.A.'
She can't keep up when I run round
And dash off in a blur.
She gets stressed out by one o'clock
(I end up supporting her).
She wears bright woolly cardigans
And skirts down to her shin.
She smells of nice deodorant
(Although it could be gin).
She can't read off the smartboard, though
From halfway down the room
I help her but I have to ask,
'Just who's supporting whom?'

Mrs. Henderson

We struggle in the science tests,
We don't like Mr. Turner
As Mrs. Henderson gets all uptight
Near any Bunsen burner.
She tries so hard at D and T,
It's clear to all for miles…
She's got a crush on Mr. Jones
And blushes when he smiles.
Last week in Art she tried to draw,
It looked like… I dare not mention.
Enough to say, it caused a scene –
The whole class got detention.

We got told off in Games, as well.
We both forgot our kit
So off we sneaked behind the sheds…
I taught her how to spit.
In music, while we sang a hymn,
I went from bad to worse.
Mrs. Henderson tried singing, too…
A very naughty verse!
The other week she had the flu
And left me on my own,
I messed about – got shouted at,
I felt totally alone.

Tickling with Words

They say that some things grow on you
(Rather like a wart)
Well Mrs. Henderson's like that,
My very own Support.
In Maths she struggles to keep up
She could ask me – but won't.
One word's enough when I play up;
Mrs. Henderson shouts 'Don't!'
We have a laugh and talk a lot,
She listens to me read.
She says I'm getting better now,
Despite my special need.
I miss her in the holidays,
With lots of words to learn.
I won't tell anyone, of course
But I'm glad when we return.
I still find lessons really hard,
My problems just won't end...
But now, with Mrs. Henderson
At least I've got a friend
Who may not know all answers yet,
And though things aren't too fine,
I look at Mrs. Henderson
And smile... because she's mine.

The end

MRS. Henderson replies...
on behalf of Teaching Assistants everywhere

They call me Mrs. Henderson,
At least, when things go well.
But often I'm called other names
Which make me blush to tell.
They call us 'The Mums' Army', too…
Each day we go to war…
The times I've rescued wounded souls
And fought with tooth and claw.

My job's 'Teaching Assistant',
They sent me on a course
And now I'm fully qualified,
With a badge that says 'Task Force'.
By and large, we rub along;
The pupils, staff and me;
With all our labels, syndromes, fears…
I keep smiling cheerfully!
Some kids are 'hyperactive'
But I am the reverse.
A morning with the little dears…
I'm comatose – or worse.

Tickling with Words

I have a job description,
Although it's quite a joke;
If I were paid for all I do,
The school would soon be broke.
I stop fights daily, lend out pens,
I listen to them read,
I dish out tissues, find lost coats,
Wipe noses when they bleed,
I fill in forms, attend reviews
And confiscate all sorts,
I coax them down from off the roof (kids and staff)
Give hugs and write reports.

Mrs. Henderson replies

I'm social worker, caretaker
(In charge of powder paint),
A skivvy, scapegoat, G.D.B. (General Dog's Body)
In short, I'm just a SAINT.
I do all this by morning break,
But then the real fun starts...
Those lunchtime squabbles need my skills
To patch up broken hearts.

I've had to deal with injuries,
I'm doctor, sister, nurse...
I'm there to mop up blood and tears
And sometimes it's far worse.
I'm asked to go on each school trip
To keep the bus intact,
Then have to lend them cash for lunch
That never gets paid back.
They cling on tight in theme park queues
Because I buy ice cream...
Then get dragged on The Nemesis...
I dodge the sick – and scream!

Mrs. Henderson replies

This term I work with Damien,
He's not an easy child.
He bears the mark of six, six, six!
When the moon is full, he's wild.
I try to show him right from wrong;
He shouts and swears and spits,
Then holds my hand and makes me cry...
For I love that child to bits.

I wonder what went on before,
When T.A.s were quite rare.
And then I fear what lies ahead...
One day I won't be there.
I only hope I've done some good;
So when they're fully-grown,
These kids will think of me and smile...
To face their world alone.

The end

Assembly
Lead in smartly...

All in straight lines
Four rows per year
Without talking
Hurry up, now

Stop that shuffling
Pick up your feet
I said, "No noise"
Fill in the gaps

This row move back
Next row lead in
Line up smartly
Stop fidgeting

Roy Briggs, keep still
That row step back
There's space down here
Stop that coughing

Assembly

Roy Briggs come here
Heads up, eyes front
Turn round, feet still
Now settle down

Who's that chewing?
Then find a bin
Yes, you right there
Get rid of it

Who's that talking?
Cut it out now
Did you hear me?
About time too

Now then, Roy Briggs
Why all the fuss?
What's so funny?
What is the joke?

Gurdeep did what?
What sort of noise?
A smelly noise?
Hush, everyone!

That's no excuse
For all that fuss
So settle down
And face this way

And Gurdeep, please
Obey the rule:
'In assembly
No blowing off.'
Sit.

The end

I don't like reading

I've joined the Public Library, which is tricky to explain
As books and reading aren't for me –
   although it helps your brain.
I said I'd like to choose a book with pictures
   about crime,
With gory, yucky, gooey bits, with action,
   blood and slime.
They stared at me in horror and took me to
   old shelves...
"Try these," they said, "they're easy books –
   just right for under-twelves."
I told them I'm a growing lad and I like action books.
They said the book on sport was out – and gave me
   grumpy looks.

Tickling with Words

I don't like reading and I don't like books,
I don't like teachers cos they give me scary looks.
I don't like libraries and I don't like school
As they're full of words and pages and they just ain't cool.

"Have you got some shorter books, I really like
'quick reads'?"
They said, "Go to the toddlers' section – or
shelves marked SPECIAL NEEDS."
I said, "I want a book on shark attacks, that's up-
to-date with fact."
The lady at the desk looked shocked, "You don't
want books like that."
She said that Dickens wrote good books and a
writer called Karl Marx,
So I said, "That's all right by me – did they write
books on sharks?"
She snapped, "You'll have to look in Reference –
for Natural History Fact."
I said, "For grisly tales of shark attacks?" She said,
"You don't want books like that."

I don't like reading

I don't like reading and I don't like books,
I don't like teachers cos they give me scary looks.
I don't like libraries and I don't like school
As they're full of words and pages and they just ain't cool.

The room was hot, the books were thick, the
   pages looked so boring…
The next I heard were whispers: "Hush – the
   library's not for snoring!"
I told her it was all so dull – she scowled at
   my remarks
So then I asked politely, "Still no picture books
   on sharks?"
She murmured words I didn't know and snapped
   so loud; "INDEED!"
Then barked "A library is for literature – you
   ought to LEARN TO READ."
So I pointed at the SILENCE sign and said,
   "You're not supposed to shout."
She sneered, she seethed, she stamped her foot
   and steaming screamed "Get Out!"

The end

(All librarians are
delightful really!)

sinking with words

I've now been doing Literacy
Each day for years at school
They give us tests and bonus points…
And treat me like a fool.

I do the same old exercise
From Green Book, chapter four
Then colour seven worksheets in…
And then I'm given more.

But if I'm good, I have a treat
And play computer games
Like 'Jack and Jill went up the hill…'
"Now you type in their names."

I match-up letters on the screen,
A 'c' makes 'cat' and 'calf'.
I try to tell the stupid thing
I'm fourteen and a half!

From time to time a man comes in
And makes me read a test:
"Tree, little, book, egg, milk…
The dog got wet and Tom had to rub him dry"…
And that means I'm assessed.

He says I've got a reading age
Of six point eight or nine,
So back I go to 'Postman Pat'
He says, "Jolly good, that's fine."

We go through vowels and consonants
Then digraphs, phonic blends,
With homonyms and suffixes…
The torture never ends.

But then the teacher, bleary-eyed
Croaks, "OK, let's adjourn."
As learner, I could teach them all…
What teachers need to learn.

It doesn't take a genius
To work out what I need;
It's someone who can give me hope
And books I WANT to read!

The end

struggling
with words

They sat me in the classroom
And said I had to wait.
They gave me sheets of paper
And said, "Now write the date."
And when I said I couldn't,
"I've got a special need."
They sat me in the corner
And gave me books to read
And when I said I couldn't,
They laughed and took the mick,
The teacher sighed and shook his head.
A kid said I was thick.
So then they said, "Fill in this form,
We have to know your name."
I said, "Well, I can TELL you that."
They said it wasn't quite the same.
They sharpened me a pencil
To write out my address
And then I said I couldn't
When the page became a mess.

A B C D E F G H I J K L M

I don't know what my problem is,
I'm lost and all at sea.
A book's a bolted, padlocked door
I just can't find the key.
The words don't click, the letters blur,
The flash cards never speak.
"Break it up and sound it out!"
They told me twice a week.
Each time I said I couldn't;
"It doesn't seem to work,"
The teacher said sarcastic things,
Then screamed and went berserk.
I can't think what the answer is,
Believe you me, I've tried
To learn that stupid alphabet...
Most nights I've sat and cried.
But still they give me spelling lists,
Stuff paper in my hand.
And still I'll feel the utter shame
Till the day they'll understand.

The end

Z Y X W V U T

N O P Q R S T

Ridiculous misadventures

Surely it couldn't get worse

It's been one of those days today...
Disastrous right from the start,
An accident-prone catastrophe-zone;
You name it, and it fell apart.
I leapt out of bed just as soon as I'd woken,
Stubbed my foot on the teapot and was rather outspoken
For the best china tea set and three toes got broken...
SURELY IT COULDN'T GET WORSE! (But it did)

It's been one of those days today...
I'm shattered and down in the dumps.
My brain is concussed, my shoulder blade's bust
And even the poodle's got mumps.
I fell out the bath, which I fractured my wrist on,
Ramming my foot down the loo, like a piston
And down on my head fell the ball-cock and cistern...
SURELY IT COULDN'T GET WORSE! (But it did)

Surely it couldn't get worse

It's been one of those days today...
Probably one of my worst.
While up in the loft, I slipped when I coughed
And somehow the water tank burst.
I fell through to next door's when I crashed through their ceiling,
Straight into their bath – and what a strange feeling,
For there sat their Nan with a cup of Darjeeling...
SURELY IT COULDN'T GET WORSE! (But it did)

Tickling with Words

It's been one of those days today...
I thought I'd re-paper the cracks...
A quick dab of paste applied with due haste,
And then I'd have time to relax.
I shot up the ladder in no time at all,
A floorboard sprang up and I started to fall;
So all that remains is the crack and no wall...
SURELY IT COULDN'T GET WORSE! (But it did)

It's been one of those days today...
Calamities round every corner;
A mass of mishaps made the greenhouse collapse
On my Grandma – with no time to warn her
So I did quick repairs at the drop of a hat
And the drop of a hammer and spanner, at that.
At last it stood firm... till a sneeze from the cat...
SURELY IT COULDN'T GET WORSE! (But it did)

It's been one of those days today...
The kitchen was needing some paint,
Just a quick touch-up, plus paper – not much up,
And all I've had since is complaint.
Aunt Mildred was coming – I had to paint faster,
But my ladder dislodged half a ton of wet plaster
That fell on dear auntie – oh what a disaster!
SURELY IT COULDN'T GET WORSE! (But it did)

It's been one of those days today...
With slip-ups and hic-cups galore.
I've bent it or managed to dent it
Or spilt purple paint on the floor.
The drain blocked-up solid so I rammed a long rod in it,
Puffin' and pantin' and pushin' and proddin' it;
You name it, I found it, unblocked it and trod in it...
SURELY IT COULDN'T GET WORSE! (But it did)

79

It's been one of those days today...
Everything's gone very wrong.
The plumbing was leaking, the water pipes squeaking...
I thought, 'No problem – it won't take too long.'
I found out the trouble – an airlock-cum-bubble
So I blew through the system full-blast at the double,
The whole lot exploded – the house is now rubble...
SURELY IT COULDN'T GET WORSE! (But it did)

It's been one of those days today...
I'm glad they're not all quite like this,
You name it, I've bashed it, just crashed it
or smashed it!
My whole life has been hit and miss.
So when you next moan at some hullabaloo,
Or when the next Friday the Thirteenth is due,
Remember there's always a loser much
worse-off than you (ME)...
(CRASH BANG WALLOP!)
WHOOPS! So yes, it could always get worse!

The end

Little Clifford Clump

Just behind the rabbit hutch
In Mrs. Clump's back yard,
Little Clifford set up camp;
The task in store quite hard.
For homework set that night was strange,
At least, so Clifford found.
It needed pickaxe and a torch
And two square yards of ground.

With toffees tucked inside his shirt
And chocolate down his socks,
He set to work with mighty blows
Amid the hollyhocks.
Digging deeper all the while
He hit a concrete pipe...
But staggered on despite the gas.
He was the stubborn type!

Little Clifford Clump

Rocks and stones and clods of mud
Lay scattered on the lawn
But Clifford shovelled ceaselessly
Until the early dawn.
Some yards beneath suburbia
Near number five's back gate,
He tunnelled 'neath the golden moon...
And the council house estate.

His pace began to slacken off,
Exhaustion soon set in...
And there he lay in sleepy state,
All brown and damp and thin.
Poor Clifford slept until disturbed
By one almighty sound...
Crashing crates and smashing glass:
This hole the milkman found.

The postman and the paperboy
Soon disappeared likewise,
With bodies, bundles, bicycles
And black eyes – what a size!
Now Mrs. Clump – she found the men,
Bedraggled in the hole
But just too late to stop the men
Delivering the coal.
With ropes they soon had clambered out,
But Clifford, in disgrace,
Was firmly told that holes weren't meant
For that particular place.
When questioned most severely
Why such a thing was done,
He answered very truthfully,
"It wasn't done for fun."

Little Clifford Clump

"My teacher recommended it
For homework set last night."
His parents wrote a strong complaint...
'Were such assignments right?'
"It's true," whined Clifford stubbornly,
"Now just you take a look.
The title's written down right here
Inside my homework book."

Now all was very soon explained
To everybody's mirth...
The title of the homework was...
"Journey To The Centre Of The Earth"
"It's literature," his mother said,
"A book by that Jules Verne,
Why must you take things literarily?
When will you ever learn?

It's a classic science fiction book."
She gave a tender smile.
But Clifford thought that digging
Was a darn sight more worthwhile.
And so, from then, the homework set
Was made extremely plain
As the English teacher had the job
Of filling that hole again.

The moral of this little tale
You may think very clear...
Not that Clifford had a clue
And his dad had no idea.
Except to say that reading books
May not, at first, seem cool
To active lads of certain age
With texts imposed at school.

Yet when a spark ignites a flame
To flash, flare and spellbind,
Lit words upon the page explode
Gunpowder of the mind.
Just light the fuse, just read the words
Just hear the laughs and screams...
Just taste the tears, just feel the power

Let books unlock your dreams!

The end

Remote-controlled underpants

For Christmas I bought a new TV remote,
Dad's old one disappeared.
I wrapped it in brand new bright Christmassy pants...
But what happened next was weird.

The glittery parcel had tinsel and bows,
Under the Christmas tree.
The fairy on top cast her spells in the night...
Dad's gift changed magically.

That TV remote and the underpants sparked,
They fizzed and fused AS ONE.
Elastic and plastic flashed super-fantastic...
The Christmas Day fun had begun.

When our presents were finally all unwrapped
My Dad was really pleased,
He put on his new pants and switched on TV...
The remote he gently squeezed.

ZAP! He tapped on a button and gasped with shock…
His pants squeezed ever so tight!
When he hit the fast-forward they spun around
At twice the speed of light.

When he pressed the red button his face turned blue
And tunes came from his chest.
He held down the pause and his pants belched out smoke
As sparks shot up his vest.

He sat down all queasy… the TV switched off,
Grey-faced, he stared in a trance…
Then Dad crossed his legs – a weird movie came on
Called 'Fifty Shades of Pants'.

When it let rip with blasts of 'Gone with the Wind'
Dad gave a startled cough
And the fairy on top of the tree blew up
The instant Dad blew off.

It was certainly a Christmas to remember.

The end

Dodgy doggerel

Crustaceans in Love
(A Lobster Quadrille)

When a lobster tried to woo a crab,
Their claws locked in a tussle.
The crab escaped an amorous grab
And the lobster pulled a mussel.

A RARE BIT of Advice

If you fancy something cheesy, here's a
  recipe that's easy;
First catch your hare — while making sure
  you firmly grab it...
Then sprinkle powdered chilli and some
  grated mild Caerphilly,
And you've got the next best thing to hot
  Welsh Rabbit.

BOSSy-Eyed

Our teacher puffs up when she shouts,
Her volume near quadruples.
Her cross-eyes bulge like brussel sprouts...
She can't control her pupils.

Not Very Punny

At school we had a competition,
Just as a bit of fun.
There'd be a prize for the best submission
Of the most hilarious pun.
A boy wrote ten and sent the lot
(He's that wimpy PIMPLY kid)
He hoped one pun might hit the SPOT
Tee hee – no pun in ten did!

Burnt to a Frazzle

A kayaker set off one night
And paddled down the river.
In bitter cold, a fire he'd light
To warm his icy shiver.
Alas, midstream, the fanned flames grew...
Be warned and don't repeat it.
He sank forever – so the saying's true;
You can't have your kayak and heat it.

Richard The Third

In case someone still hasn't heard,
(And though it may sound quite absurd)
A corpse left to fester
In a car park in Leicester
Was His Majesty, Richard the Third...
Who was dug up, wiped down and interred.
(In Leicester Cathedral in 2015 – after
  paying a king-size parking fine).

Einstein

Doctor Einstein must surely be right;
If you travel much faster than light.
You'd zoom off today
In a Relative Way,
And return by ten thirty last night.

Carnivorous Vegetarian

Some animals are cannibals and so is
    my young cousin,
She'll eat men made of gingerbread
    and babies by the dozen (jelly ones)
Tiger-like, she'll pounce on them with
    fierce blood-curdling roars
Then bite each head off one by one to
    crush between her jaws.
The gooey bits burst out and squelch
    with every dribbling bite;
She licks her lips and wipes her chin
    and purrs with sheer delight.
You'd think she was a tiger if you'd
    never heard her purr before…
She growls dismembering broccoli –
    a homicidal herbivore!

Who am I?

I'm ENORMOUSLY strong and intelligent
And, though you might think it's irrelevant,
My memory's splendid.
Now my riddle is ended
And I'll never forget I'm an elephant.
Oops, I forgot you had to guess who I was!

Hairy Mary

There was an old lady called Mary
Whose face was exceptionally hairy.
She said, "It's not weird
That I've got a long beard...
It's my green furry body that's scary."

Apples Limerick

A woman from East of Kilbride
Ate ninety-six apples and died.
From over-indulging,
Her gut began bulging...
Brewing cider inside her insides.

Please don't mention it

I gave my Dad an elephant,
I stole her from the zoo.
She wasn't very elegant
And caused a hullabaloo.
Dad locked her in the closet
Where we built a large extension,
But she left a huge deposit
Which we're not allowed to mention.
"Forget she's there and never say,
Just go and get the broom."
Swept under the carpet to this day
Is the elephant in the room.

Pun Time: Playing with words

Some people think that playwrights
Are dull and boring nerds,
But my pantomime was packed with puns...
A witty play on words.

They offered me a brain transplant,
As I'm falling far behind
In all my studies – so I agreed...
And now I've changed my mind.

My friend's annoying puns on birds
Are bad and all the same.
I told him I was not EMUsed...
Yes, toucan play that game.

A frog parked his sports car at the side of
  the road,
By a meter – but the frog didn't pay.
He hopped off in flip-flops – bright green
  open-toad…
Guess wart? He got frog-marched off –
and his car toad away.

I'm really bad at woodwork,
I made a bookcase frame
Then all the books fell on my head…
I've only got myshelf to blame.

I've tried to write a lot of puns
To make you laugh and smirk;
The ones about bone-idle kids…
I still can't make them work!

The invisible invisible string

'To be, or not to be',
that is the existentialist thread...

Has anyone seen my invisible thread?
It's got to be somewhere round here.
I left it on top of the thingamajig...
How can invisible thread disappear?
I got it to tie up an oojamaflip,
A doodah and thingamabob...
The whatchamecallit shouldn't be seen,
So that thread was just right for the job.

The last time I used some invisible thread
The dog ate a couple of metres.
It wouldn't have mattered – but out in the street,
It blew-off and lassoed Mrs Peters.
The cat chewed the end and swallowed a chunk,
Then climbed to the top of the ladder
Where a workman was sanding the dusty high walls...
The cat sneezed – and sewed-up his bladder.

Has anyone seen my invisible thread?
Surely it's not disappeared.
They ought to supply it with luminous ends...
Has it vanished forever? How weird.
Unless – here's a thought – it might never have come,
Though costing a fortune online,
When the package arrived, was it empty inside?
Yikes – I've been stitched-up by imaginary twine!

Despite little proof, I had faith all was real;
Loose ends neatly tied up and twisted,
Yet if I'm mistaken, my belief has been shaken
For what if it never existed?
Perhaps I've been hoodwinked, bamboozled or conned,
Or just strung along – well how numbing...
I bought non-existent philosophical thread
And, what's more, did not see it coming!

The end

In case you didn't know, invisible thread is often used for tricks. It is a very thin nylon strand that can't be seen easily and is used by illusionists to make small objects seem to fly... possibly!

Psst – it's a secret
(shhhh)

Psst – you've really got to listen,
Psst – you've really got to hear…
Psst – just let me whisper carefully
A message in your ear.

Psst – it's really very secret
Psst – it's really special, too
Psst – it's really so important…
A message that is true.

Psst – I really need to tell you
Psst – you really need to know
Psst – just pay attention carefully…
A message – here we go:

"Psss wersss wiss pursss swish swish zip
Psss wersss wiss pursss swish swish zwatt
Psss wersss wiss pursss swish swish zip."
That's the lot so now you know –
    I hope you got all that!"

My words get passed right down the line
From ear to mouth to ear…
They think it's Chinese whispers BUT
They're not all meant to hear!

Psst – it's meant to be a secret
Psst – you weren't supposed to tell
Psst – now everybody's pointing…
Psst – they're sniggering as well.

Psst – You weren't supposed to pass it on,
You've now told everyone!
The message was for you alone:
Psst – 'You left your zip UNDONE'.

Psst – This message of embarrassment
Could somehow be far worse…
Imagine if it went worldwide
In a Cheesy Book of Verse (psst – it just has!)

The end

Tickling with Words

Glossary

Cyanide A poison lethal to humans.

Emu A large, flightless Australian bird that can run at high speeds.

Fair Dinkum An Australian turn of phrase, used to emphasise that something is true.

Incisors The narrow-edged teeth used for cutting at the front of the mouth.

Jules Verne A Victorian science-fiction writer, famous for novels including *Journey to the Centre of the Earth* and *20,000 Leagues Under The Sea.*

Mothballs Smelly lumps of material placed in clothing to keep away moths who might eat the fabric.

Nylon A synthetic thread-like material used to make artificial clothing and other products.

Oliver Twist The title character of a novel by Charles Dickens.

He is a street orphan in Victorian London who turns to a life of crime.

Quadrille A type of music played during a square dance of the same name, which usually involves four couples dancing in a rectangular formation.

Tranquillisers Drugs used to knock out animals or people who are behaving aggressively or violently.

Vampire Mythical creatures – humans who have returned from the dead to drink the blood of the living.

Werewolves Mythical creatures – humans who transform into giant wolf-like creatures during a full moon.

Zombie Mythical creatures – humans who have returned from the dead as moaning, shuffling, flesh-eating monsters.